D1226370

LIFE *on* EARTH

MAKING SENSE *of* SCIENCE

Peter Riley

A+

Smart Apple Media

First published in 2004 by Franklin Watts
96 Leonard Street, London EC2A 4XD

Franklin Watts Australia
45–51 Huntley Street, Alexandria NSW 2015

Series editor: Rachel Cooke, Editor: Kate Newport,
Art director: Jonathan Hair, Designer: Mo Choy

Picture credits:
Ancient Art & Architecture Collection/Topham: 7t. Ian Beames/Ecoscene: 19cl.
J.L. Carson/Custom Medical Stock/Science Photo Library: 14cl.
Nigel Cattlin/Holt Studios: 24b.
Bruce Coleman Collection: front cover, 1. Vicki Coombs/Ecoscene: 16c.
A.B. Dowsett/Science Photo Library: 11tr.
Pascal Goetgheluck/Science Photo Library: 18t.
Chinch Gryniewiz/Ecoscene: 17t, 20l. Ian Harwood/Ecoscene: 22b.
James Kings-Holmes/Science Photo Library: 14b.
Michael Howes/Ecoscene: 21b.
Michael Howes/Garden Picture Library/Alamy: 26.
Rosemary Mayer/Holt Studios: 25t.
Astrid & Hanns-Frieder Michler/Science Photo Library: 11cl.
Neeraj Mishra/Ecoscene: 29b. Sally Morgan/Ecoscene: 25b.
Natural History Museum, London: 6b.
Robert Pickett/Ecoscene: 19tr. Picturepoint/Topham: 9t. Carlos Sanz/Ecoscene: 23b.
Sinclair Stammers/Science Photo Library: 10t. Superstock/Alamy: 22tr.
Andrew Syred/Science Photo Library: 10c, 17b.
Geoff Tompkinson/Science Photo Library: 15b.
WG/Science Photo Library: 5b. Mike Whittle/Ecoscene: 6t.

All other photography by Ray Moller.

Published in the United States by Smart Apple Media
2140 Howard Drive West, North Mankato, Minnesota 56003

Library of Congress Cataloging-in-Publication Data

Riley, Peter D.
Life on Earth / by Peter Riley.
p. cm. — (Making sense of science)
Includes index.
ISBN 1-58340-714-6
1. Biology—Juvenile literature. I. Title.

QH309.2.R55 2005
570—dc22   2004059971

2 4 6 8 9 7 5 3 1

CONTENTS

SIGNS OF LIFE

People have always needed other living things. We need plants and animals for our food, our clothes, and many of our medicines. We even rely on plants to make the oxygen we breathe (see pages 20–21). Because living things are essential to us, it is important that we study and understand them.

THE SEVEN FEATURES OF LIFE

How do we tell if something is living or not? This may seem like a silly question, but sometimes it is hard to be sure.

Scientists have identified seven features or characteristics that all living things have. Non-living things may have some of these characteristics, but only living things have all seven.

MOVEMENT

All living things move in some way. It is easy to see that animals move. Plants also move, but much more slowly; plant leaves slowly change position to face the sun, and flowers often open during the day and close at night.

SENSITIVITY

Living things are aware of their surroundings and respond to them to stay alive. We call this sensitivity.

FEEDING

All living things need food. They use materials from food to maintain their bodies, to grow, and to get energy. Animals get their food by eating plants or other animals. Plants make their own food using materials from the air and soil, and energy from sunlight.

RESPIRATION

Animals and plants need oxygen to unlock the energy stored in food. The process of releasing energy from food is called respiration. Animals and plants living on land get oxygen from the air. Oxygen also dissolves in water, so living things in the oceans or in fresh water take in oxygen from the water.

EXCRETION

The process of living and growing produces waste products that are harmful and must be removed. Removing these wastes is called excretion. In humans and many animals, the lungs remove a waste gas called carbon dioxide from the body, while the kidneys remove wastes from the blood.

REPRODUCING

When a living thing is fully grown, it becomes capable of reproducing (producing young).

GROWING

Living things grow by increasing in size, but they can also change completely as they grow. For instance, tadpoles change into frogs, and caterpillars turn into butterflies.

CAN YOU REVIVE AN ONION?

An onion can sit unchanged in your cupboard for weeks, but what happens to it if it is warm and receives water? Set an onion on top of a container of water and set it in a warm place. What happens?

LIFE FROM WATER

The ancient Greeks noticed that there were many kinds of life in water and believed that this is where life first developed. Fossils were first thought to be stones that resembled living things. When scientists discovered that fossils were really the remains of ancient plants and animals, they found they could use them to learn more about where living things came from. As they looked at older and older fossils, they found that the first living things did in fact live in water as the ancient Greeks believed.

OBSERVING AND RECORDING

Scientists known as ecologists study living things in their surroundings by making observations and recording them. Living things are found almost everywhere on Earth. They can survive in the bitter cold of the polar regions and the dry heat of the desert. In less extreme conditions, such as forests and coral reefs, there is a huge variety of life. In every habitat, living things have adapted so that they can survive, breed, and raise young.

This photo shows a group of ecologists studying a colony of emperor penguins in Antarctica.

RECORDING WHAT IS SEEN

The simplest way of studying a living thing is to look at its body and note its features. These observations can be used along with observations about its life to see how the living thing has adapted to survive in its surroundings.

When scientists observe the features of a living thing, they make a detailed drawing to highlight the important features. This is an exact drawing of a song thrush.

KEEP LOOKING

Ecologists may study and record the movements of living things over many days, months, or years and keep their notes in a diary. The information helps to build up a detailed account of how living things survive in their habitats. If the living thing is a plant, the time at which it flowers may be noted, and this may be related to the weather conditions and temperature. If the living thing is an animal, its feeding habits may be found to change at certain times of the year.

CATS AND DOGS

Can you tell a cat from a dog just from careful observation? Look at a cat and a dog and note their different features. Look at their heads, their bodies, and their behavior. Now look at some other cats and dogs. Which of the features you noted are useful for telling dogs and cats apart, and which are found in both dogs and cats?

BUILDING OBSERVATIONS

Visit a park regularly and keep a diary of the plants and animals you see. Note the weather conditions on your visits. After a month, look through your notes and see if the information you have collected tells you anything about how weather affects plants and animals in the park.

The aurochs, a kind of wild ox, is one of the three most common animals shown in the cave paintings near Lascaux, France.

About 17,000 years ago, people living in what is now France painted animals on the walls of caves. It is thought that the paintings were made to bring the people luck when they hunted. These paintings were so detailed that we can recognize most of the animals. They also feature animals that are now extinct, such as the aurochs (a large, wild ox), and animals that are no longer found in Europe, such as the rhino.

SORTING OUT LIVING THINGS

The Greek thinker Aristotle (384–322 B.C.) was a good observer and described many forms of life. He was one of the first scientists to group, or classify, life-forms. He tried to order them in what he called a "great chain." At the top was the ultimate form of being, God, and at the bottom were non-living things. He sub-divided the groups in between these two extremes as well, paying particular attention to detail in animals. He noticed, for instance, that when dolphins give birth, they produce a placenta (see page 19), like cattle and sheep. Fish did not do this, so he correctly grouped dolphins with cattle and sheep rather than with fish.

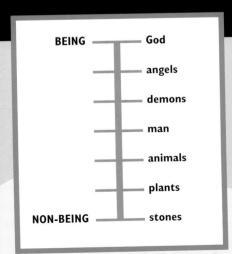

BEING —— God
—— angels
—— demons
—— man
—— animals
—— plants
NON-BEING —— stones

Aristotle's great chain ordered both living and non-living things, from stones to humans, in one line.

CLASSIFYING LIVING THINGS

When your bedroom becomes messy, you sort it out, putting books in one place, toys in another, and so on. In a similar way, scientists from Aristotle onward have tried to sort out the millions of different kinds of living things by classifying them. Today, different living things are sorted into groups according to the features they have in common.

THE PLANT KINGDOM

The biggest groupings of living things are called kingdoms. Each kingdom is divided into smaller groups. The plant kingdom is divided into four groups: flowering plants, cone-bearers or conifers, ferns, and mosses and liverworts.

PLANT KINGDOM

FLOWERING PLANTS
flowers;
seeds form in fruits.

CONE-BEARERS
needle-like leaves;
seeds form in cones.

FERNS
make spores, not seeds;
made on underside of leaves.

MOSSES AND LIVERWORTS
make spores, not seeds;
tiny leaves.

THE ANIMAL KINGDOM

The animal kingdom is divided broadly as invertebrates (animals without a backbone) and vertebrates (animals with a backbone). There are many invertebrate groups, such as insects, crustaceans, mollusks, jellyfish, and starfish. There are five vertebrate groups: fish, amphibians, reptiles, birds, and mammals.

FEATURES IN COMMON

All of the living things in a particular group have certain features in common. For example, an animal that has scaly skin and lays eggs on land is placed in the reptile group. However, there are many different kinds of reptiles, such as turtles, crocodiles, snakes, and lizards. So the reptile group is divided into smaller groups. Each of these groups is divided again into even smaller groups, and so on down to individual species (kinds) of animals or plants.

VERTEBRATES

FISH
scaly skin;
gills;
live in water.

AMPHIBIANS
smooth skin;
young live in water.

REPTILES
scaly skin;
lay eggs with shells.

BIRDS
skin covered by feathers;
wings and beak;
shelled eggs.

MAMMALS
hairy or furry;
female feeds young
breast milk.

To show how these groupings work, here is the classification for a particular reptile, the Nile crocodile.

Group	Name of group
Kingdom	Animal
Phylum	Vertebrates
Class	Reptiles
Order	Crocodiles and alligators
Family	Crocodiles
Genus	*Crocodylus*
Species	*niloticus*

The last two groupings of the Nile crocodile, its genus and species, together make up its scientific name: *Crocodylus niloticus*. Scientific names are made from Latin and Greek words. They may seem complicated, but the advantage of the names is that scientists around the world understand them, no matter what language they speak. They also identify a particular species, even if it is known by different names in different areas or countries.

This portrait shows Linnaeus during a trip to collect plants in Lapland in 1732.

The classification of living things we use today was developed from the work of Carolus Linnaeus (1707–1778), a Swedish botanist. He traveled widely, studying plants and putting them into groups. He arranged them in large groups called classes, then divided each class into smaller groups. Linnaeus started the practice of giving every living thing a scientific name. This was made up of the genus and species names and based on Latin and Greek words.

INSECTS AND SPIDERS

Insects have six legs, and spiders have eight. Can you find both kinds of animals on a branch? Place a plastic sheet under a small tree branch, then shake it or hit it with a stick. Look at the animals that fall onto the sheet: are there any insects or spiders? When you have finished, put the sheet close to the tree trunk so the animals can climb back up the tree.

Although all insects have six legs, you will find differences between them. Look for differences in body shape, the length of the legs, and the size and shape of the wings (if any).

This is what was collected from an apple tree. You might find insects, spiders, and even snails.

LOOKING AT MICROBES

Microbes are forms of life that are so small we cannot see them with the naked eye. We need a microscope to see them. As with larger forms of life, scientists have observed microscopic living things closely in order to classify them. Some microbes have similarities to larger living things, but others are quite different.

SMALLER COUSINS

Some of the larger forms of microscopic life are close relatives of other much larger animals. Some crustaceans (animals such as crabs and shrimps) are microscopic. One example is a tiny creature called a daphnia.

Under a microscope, light shines through a *daphnia*'s transparent body, and its intestines can be seen.

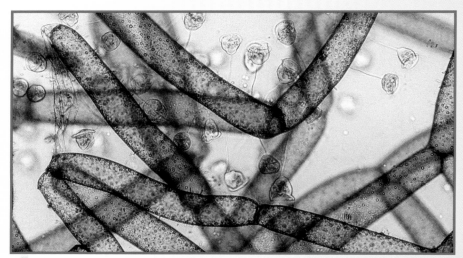

These tiny green algae have been magnified many times under the microscope. Most algae live in fresh water, but some live in the sea.

ALGAE

Pond water is clear in winter, but when conditions become warmer and brighter, the water often turns green. This is because billions of microscopic, plant-like microbes called algae grow in the water.

FLOAT OR SINK?

Algae have drops of oil inside their bodies. How might this help them stay in the sunlit, upper waters of a pond? Put some cooking oil in an eye dropper. Put the tip of the eye dropper into a glass of water and squeeze the rubber end. What happens to the oil drops when they enter the water?

PROTISTS

Some forms of microscopic pond life are covered in tiny hairs and move quickly through the water. They are called ciliates, and they belong to a group of microbes called protists. Another group of protists have a long, whip-like hair to help them move. Many protists feed on algae or on protists smaller than themselves.

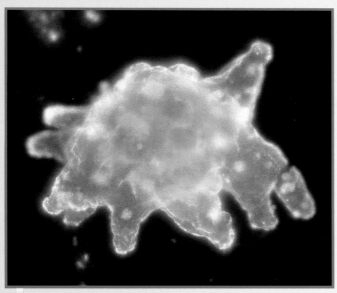

This is an amoeba, which belongs to the group of microbes called protists. Its body flows over surfaces by constantly changing shape.

BACTERIA

Bacteria are much smaller than other microbes. A very powerful microscope called an electron microscope is needed to see them clearly. Bacteria are found almost everywhere. Many feed by breaking down the remains of other living things (see page 26). Other bacteria live on or in the bodies of animals or humans. Most of the time, we don't notice them, but occasionally some kinds of bacteria invade the body and cause disease.

These bacteria are found in our digestive tract.

THE FIRST SIGHT OF MICROBES

Antonie van Leeuwenhoek (1632–1723), a Dutch biologist, made many simple but powerful microscopes. His design had only one lens, but the most powerful versions could magnify more than 250 times. He examined many different samples, including human spit and water in which grass had been allowed to rot. From his work, he discovered protists and bacteria.

FUNGI

We tend to think of mushrooms and toadstools when we think of fungi, but there are other fungi, such as molds, that are considered to be microbes. Most fungi produce microscopic, seed-like spores that can travel on the smallest air currents. When they settle on a suitable food, the spores grow a network of microscopic feeding threads. When there are enough of them, these threads can be seen with the naked eye. We call them mold.

FEEDING FUNGI

Put some fruit and cheese in a screw-top jar. Put the lid on loosely and check the jar over the next week or so. Can you see the feeding threads of molds developing on the food?

UNITS OF LIFE

The parts from which living bodies are made are called organs. If you took a very thin slice of an organ and looked at it with a microscope, you would find that the organ is made up of millions of tiny packets of life called cells.

WHAT'S IN A CELL?

Nearly all cells have three basic parts—a nucleus, cytoplasm, and a cell membrane. The nucleus is a large, darker spot in the middle of each cell. It contains the cell's genetic material. The cytoplasm is a grainy, jelly-like material around the nucleus, while the cell membrane is the thin outer layer that holds the cell together.

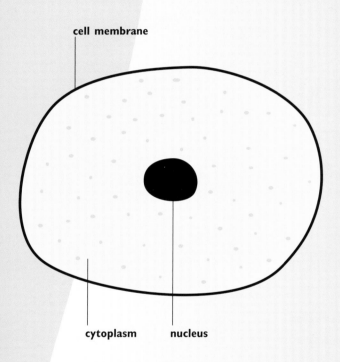

cell membrane

cytoplasm   nucleus

Animal cells have a nucleus, cytoplasm, and a cell membrane.

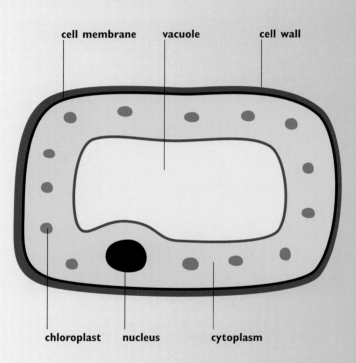

cell membrane   vacuole   cell wall

chloroplast   nucleus   cytoplasm

Plant cells have three more features than animal cells —a thick wall for extra support, a cavity within the cell containing a watery solution called a vacuole, and chloroplasts, which trap energy from sunlight and use it to make food.

TISSUES AND ORGANS

Cells do not just pack together in a disorderly way. Groups of similar cells, called tissues, grow and work together to perform a certain task in the body. Groups of tissues grow and work together in organs.

CAN YOU SEE THE CELLS?

Peel off a thin strip of onion skin. Place it on a flat piece of clear plastic and hold it up to a window (make sure the sun is not shining directly through). Look at the skin with a magnifying glass. You should see many tiny cells.

Leaves are probably the most important organs in plants. A leaf takes in energy from sunlight, draws up water from the plant's roots, and takes in carbon dioxide from the air. Inside the leaf cells, these ingredients are put together to make sugary food.

Transparent cells on the leaf's surface let in light. These cells have a waxy surface to stop water from escaping.

Tightly packed cells containing large numbers of chloroplasts (palisade cells) trap energy from sunlight and use it to make food.

Loosely packed, spongy mesophyll cells allow water vapor and carbon dioxide to circulate in the air spaces between them. Water and carbon dioxide are essential parts of the plant's food-making process (see pages 20-21).

Veins running through the leaf bring water from the roots to the leaf and take sugary sap from the leaf to other parts of the plant.

Holes in the lower surface of the leaf allow air in and out. Around each hole are two cells that can bend or straighten to open or close the hole.

THE SMALLEST LIVING THINGS

The smallest living things, such as algae, protists, and bacteria, have a body made from just one cell. The parts of these cells, such as the hairs in protists, are not called organs but organelles.

WHO **THOUGHT THEM** UP?

The words "cell" and "nucleus" came from the ideas of two scientists after they had made observations under a microscope.

Robert Hooke (1635–1703), an English scientist, looked at a very thin slice of cork under a microscope and saw that it was made up of tiny compartments. He gave them the name "cells" because he thought they looked like the cells of monks in a monastery.

When Robert Brown (1773–1858), a Scottish scientist, looked at plant cells under a microscope, he saw that they all had a dark spot in them. (Hooke did not see dark spots in his cells because cork is dead tissue.) The shape of each spot reminded him of a nut, so he called the spot the "nucleus," which means "a little nut."

HOW NEW CELLS ARE MADE

Cells renew themselves by dividing in two. This is how living things grow. Under our skin, for instance, we have a layer of cells that divides constantly. The cells are pushed to the skin's surface, where they are eventually rubbed away. (The flakes of skin that are rubbed off make up much of the dust in your home and school.) The skin provides a protective cover to the body, and the dividing cells make sure that it is not worn away.

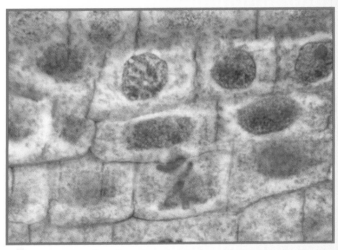

In the tip of a plant root is an area where cells divide rapidly. You can see this happening near the bottom of this photo.

SEEING ROOT HAIR CELLS

Get some dried beans and soak one overnight. Line the sides of a clear plastic drinking cup with blotting paper or paper towel. Hold the blotting paper in place by putting a wad of cotton in the bottom of the cup. Pour in about a half an inch (1 cm) of water. Push the bean between the blotting paper and the glass wall. Watch its root grow every day. When the sides of the root seem fuzzy, look at them with a magnifying glass. Each hair you see is a cell growing out from the root by the process of cell division.

STUDYING PEA PLANTS

Gregor Mendel (1822–1884) was an Austrian monk who investigated pea plants in the monastery garden. He found that if he controlled how the flowers were pollinated, he could predict what features would appear in the next generation of plants. From this, he figured out that instructions were passed on from one generation to the next. He called these instructions "factors." Today, we call them genes. They are composed of DNA.

Today, Mendel is seen as the founder of the science of genetics, but his work was not recognized in his lifetime.

COPYING CHROMOSOMES

As a cell prepares to divide, threads appear in the nucleus. They are called chromosomes, and they contain the genetic material. Each chromosome makes a copy of itself. The chromosomes and their copies separate and enter the two new nuclei so that each new nucleus has a set of genetic material to help it develop and stay alive.

CHROMOSOMES AND DNA

The chromosomes are made of molecules called DNA. The DNA molecule is an immensely long double chain twisted into a spiral shape. Chemicals called bases are arranged along this chain. The order of the bases along the chain forms a code that gives instructions to the cell and controls the way it grows and develops.

DNA FINGERPRINTING

Have you ever dropped water on an ink spot and watched the colors separate on the surrounding paper? A similar but more complicated process of separation can be applied to DNA taken from the cells in the saliva or blood of a person. When the DNA is allowed to separate, it forms bands like a long bar code. Each person's pattern of bands is unique and can be used like a fingerprint for identification.

The DNA molecule is made up of two long chains that are joined together by pairs of bases. Bases are called alanine (dark green), thymine (light green), guanine (dark blue), and cytosil (light blue). The double chain is twisted into a spiral shape.

A laboratory technician looking at a DNA "fingerprint."

CELLS THAT MAKE NEW PLANTS

Some cells in plants and animals are specially designed to join with a cell from another plant or animal of the same kind to make a new individual. These cells are called sex cells, or gametes. The gametes are made in the reproductive organs. Here we look at how flowering plants reproduce (reproduction in animals is explained on pages 18–19).

THE PARTS OF A FLOWER

The flower is the part of the plant that contains the reproductive organs. The male reproductive organs are called stamens. They produce many tiny pollen grains, each of which contains a male gamete. The female reproductive organs are called ovules. Each one contains an egg cell, which is the female gamete. The ovules are enclosed in an ovary, which has a surface called a stigma at its top.

stigma

stamen
(makes pollen grains)

ovary
(contains ovules)

LOOK INSIDE SOME FLOWERS

Look at some flowers and see if you can see the stamens, stigma, and ovary. Some flowers, such as the buttercup, have many small ovaries, each with a stigma. Plants such as dandelions, daisies, and sunflowers produce large numbers of flowers, each with just one petal. These are grouped together on a stalk to form a flower head.

POLLINATION

Pollination is a process in which pollen travels from one flower to another. The pollen may be transferred by insects, as in the sweet pea, or by wind, as in grass plants. The pollen travels from the stamen of one plant's flower to the stigma of a flower on another plant of the same species.

Insect-pollinated flowers are often colorful and scented to attract insects. Wind-pollinated flowers often have small, green flowers. When their pollen is ready, they hang out their stamens so the wind can blow it away.

Grasses are wind-pollinated plants. These grasses have their stamens hanging out of the flower.

CAN YOU SEE THE POLLEN?

Look at the pollen of wind- and insect-pollinated flowers. Dab the stamens of each type of flower onto a slide and look at them under a microscope. The pollen carried by insects has spikes on it to help the grains attach to the insect's body. The pollen carried by the wind has smooth surfaces.

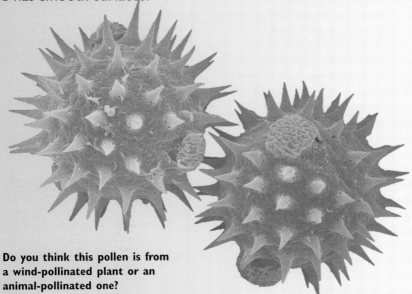

Do you think this pollen is from a wind-pollinated plant or an animal-pollinated one?

FERTILIZATION

After pollination, a tube grows from the pollen grain into the ovary until it reaches an ovule. The male gamete travels down the pollen tube, enters the ovule, and fuses with the female gamete in a process called fertilization. A new cell is produced with chromosomes from its two parent plants. This cell forms the beginning of a new plant, while other tissues in the ovule make a seed.

The ovary forms a fruit that helps the seeds disperse. When the seeds land in a suitable place, they germinate and grow into new plants.

ANIMAL REPRODUCTION

Like plants, animals produce sex cells, or gametes. The male sex cell is called the sperm, and the female sex cell is called the egg. Male animals produce sperm cells, and females produce egg cells.

HOW A NEW ANIMAL FORMS

A new animal is formed when the nucleus of a sperm cell fuses with the nucleus of an egg cell. The cell with this new nucleus is called a zygote. It then divides like ordinary body cells. The new cells produced continue to divide, and in time, a new animal begins to form.

FERTILIZATION

The joining of the nucleus of a sperm to the nucleus of an egg is called fertilization. There are two kinds of fertilization in animals. Fertilization may take place outside the bodies of the parents. This is called external fertilization. Frogs and many fish reproduce in this way. In other animals, fertilization takes place inside the body of the female. This is called internal fertilization. It occurs in insects, some fish, reptiles, birds, and mammals.

EGGS

The familiar object we call an egg, such as a chicken egg, is different than a fertilized egg cell (zygote). The egg cell is deep inside the egg, surrounded by several protective layers. Eggs

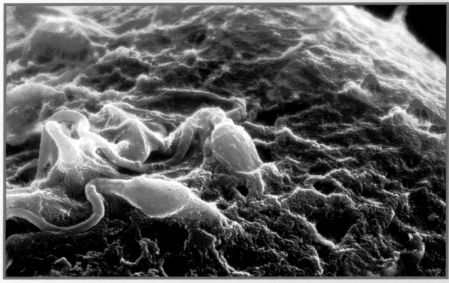

Two sperm on the surface of an egg cell. Only one of the sperm that reach the egg cell will fertilize it.

also contain food so that the zygote can grow. This is what we call the yolk. The eggs we buy in stores are unfertilized—they do not contain a growing chick.

Birds have hard-shelled eggs, but the eggs of some reptiles, such as turtles, have a leathery shell.

WHAT'S IN AN EGG?

Break open a chicken egg and look at the parts. The shell provides protection, and at one end there is an air space for respiration. The white provides water, the stabilizers keep the yolk from turning around, and the yolk provides food for the developing embryo.

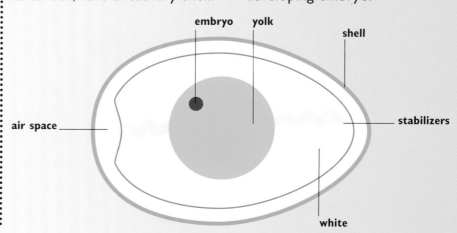

A MAMMAL'S EARLY LIFE

In mammals, the fertilized egg grows inside the mother's body. It grows first into an embryo. As it gets bigger, it is called a fetus. The fetus gets food and removes waste through an organ called the placenta. The placenta is attached to the wall of the mother's womb. It takes nourishment from the mother's blood and passes it to the fetus. It also passes waste from the fetus into the mother's blood.

When the fetus is ready to be born, the walls of the womb push it down the birth canal to the outside world.

Butterflies and many other insects undergo metamorphosis.

Sheep are mammals. The lamb lives and grows inside its mother's womb before being born at a relatively late stage of development. The young then feed on milk from their mothers until they are ready to survive without it.

GROWTH AND CHANGE

After birth or hatching, many animals grow and change but remain basically the same (see left). But a few animals—such as insects and amphibians—start off in one young form, then change into different-looking adults. For instance, butterflies begin life as caterpillars, then change to their adult form later. Likewise, a tadpole transforms into a frog. This change is called metamorphosis.

WHERE DO FLIES COME FROM?

If you leave out some meat, maggots may soon appear in it. This observation led many people to believe that living things could develop from non-living materials. Francesco Redi (1626–1697), an Italian doctor, investigated this idea by leaving out two plates of meat. One he covered, and the other he left uncovered so flies could feed on it. He found that maggots developed only in the uncovered meat. Redi had shown that flies had to lay eggs on the meat for maggots to grow in it.

HOW PLANTS MAKE FOOD

Life on Earth depends on light energy from the sun. Plants take in part of the light energy that reaches them and use it to make food. Plants also need water and minerals from the soil, and carbon dioxide from the air for this process. It is called photosynthesis.

A tree's leaves are arranged so that they overlap as little as possible. This allows each leaf to get the maximum amount of sunlight.

The organ of the plant that makes food is the leaf. It is made of several kinds of cells arranged into tissues that carry out this task (see pages 12–13). The light-grabbing substance in plants is called chlorophyll. It is found in little granules called chloroplasts inside the leaf cells.

PLANTS AND LIGHT

How does light affect the health of a plant? Put some bean seedlings in a dark place and keep some other bean seedlings in a sunlit place. After a few days, look at the two sets of beans. The bean plants kept in the dark will grow spindly and become less green.

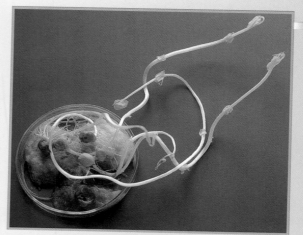

These spindly bean shoots were grown in the dark.

GETTING RAW MATERIALS

Leaves get the water they need through the plant's roots. The roots take in water from the soil, and it travels up thin tubes from the roots to the leaves.

Leaves have many tiny holes in them that let the plant take in carbon dioxide from the air. These are usually in the lower surface so that the plant does not lose too much water through the holes in strong sunlight. The energy from sunlight is then used to change the carbon dioxide and water into a food (carbohydrate) and a gas (oxygen). The oxygen then passes out of the leaf into the air.

GETTING CARBON DIOXIDE

Inside a leaf, the concentration of carbon dioxide is low because it is constantly being used up to make food. In the air outside, the concentration of carbon dioxide is higher, and the gas moves into the leaf by a process known as diffusion.

DIFFUSION IN ACTION

To see diffusion in action, put some warm water in a clear bowl and let it settle. Put a drop of food coloring into the water at one edge of the bowl. Over the next few hours, watch the colored region spread out by diffusion.

CROP PRODUCTION

Once scientists discovered how plants make food, they began to look at ways of using this knowledge to improve the production of crops. Since plants need carbon dioxide from the air and nutrients from the soil, extra supplies of both are added in greenhouses so that a crop of food can be grown as large as possible.

Joannes Baptiste van Helmont (1577–1644), a Flemish (Belgian) scientist, believed that a plant needed only water and light to grow. He weighed a young tree and the soil it was to grow in, then provided the plant with only water and sunlight for the next five years. When he weighed the tree and soil again, he found that the tree had increased in mass by 160 pounds (73 kg) while the soil had lost 2 ounces (60 g). These results suggested that a little soil was needed, but that the rest of the new growth must have been due to water. However, plant material was known to contain carbon, and water does not contain carbon. Jan Ingenhousz (1730–1799), a Dutch scientist, showed that carbon dioxide in the air is absorbed by plants when light shines on them. This formed the link between the air and how plants make food.

After it was found that warmth increased a plant's food production, farmers began to grow crops in greenhouses.

LIVING TOGETHER

A living thing cannot survive on its own. It depends on other living things for its survival. Living things live together in groups called communities. The place where a community lives is called a habitat. Sometimes plants and animals in the same habitat compete for food, water, space, or (if they are plants) light. Food, water, space, and light are known as a habitat's resources.

MAKE A WATERY HABITAT

If you keep fish, you have already created a watery habitat for them. However, you can easily set up a simple community in water with gravel, water plants, and snails (purchased from a store that sells aquariums and fish). Look at the community regularly and keep a diary of what you see. How does the community change over a few weeks?

INSECT POLLINATORS

On a sunny day, sit near some flowers and trees and record the different kinds of insects that visit them. You might see butterflies, hoverflies, bees, and perhaps beetles.

HELPING EACH OTHER

The living things in a community help each other survive in a variety of ways. One obvious way is as food. Plants or plant parts are food for many animals, while other animals eat the plant-eaters. Plants can also provide shelter. Holes in trees may be used by nesting birds and roosting bats, while deer may find shelter in bushes.

Plants can also benefit from animals. Many plants depend on insects to spread pollen, which enables the flower to reproduce. In return, the insects get to feed on sweet nectar from the flowers they pollinate.

Some plants use animals to help disperse their seeds. They produce succulent fruit with indigestible seeds. Animals eat the fruit, but the seeds pass through the animals' bodies unharmed and reach the ground with a supply of manure that helps them grow.

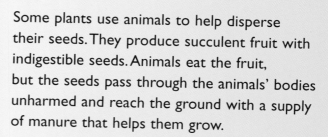

COMPETITION

Sometimes living things compete for the things they need. If numbers of a particular kind of bird become too great, there may not be enough food or nesting places for all of them, and some will move to other habitats. Plants cannot move, but they can compete for space and water. When this happens, some plants may not grow well or may die.

NOT ENOUGH ROOM

Plant some seeds close together in a seed tray. Plant some more seeds with large spaces between them in a second seed tray. Water both trays and put them in a sunny place. Record how the plants grow. You should find that the plants with more space between them grow better.

Sometimes large areas of land that have been used for mining or industry are no longer needed. Instead of letting the buildings slowly fall down, materials such as metals are stripped from them for recycling, and the buildings are demolished. The rubble is bulldozed into small hills, and parts of the ground may be dug out to make lakes or ponds. The soil that is dug out is used to cover the rubble, and grass seed is sown in it. Ecologists select plants that will grow in the new environment and set up a habitat that will attract animals. Insects and birds are attracted to flowers and fruits, while frogs and dragonflies are attracted to ponds. Even rabbits, foxes, and deer may move in. Blinds may be set up so people can watch the wildlife without disturbing them. Habitat construction like this helps conserve wildlife and educates people about the living world.

DANCING BEES

Ecologists build up knowledge about animals and plants by very careful observation. Karl von Frisch (1886–1982), an Austrian zoologist, observed bees on their honeycomb. He saw that they performed dances in which they moved around and wiggled their bodies. He discovered that these movements told other bees about the direction and distance of flowers that were producing nectar.

A bee doing a wiggle dance makes two loops with a straight run in the middle. The straight run is in the direction of the food source.

FOOD CHAINS AND WEBS

An animal cannot make its own food, so it must get it from plants or other animals. Animals that feed on plants are called herbivores, while animals that feed on other animals are called carnivores. Animals that eat both plant and animal food are called omnivores. Each animal is adapted to feed in a certain way. The movement of food from plants to herbivores and then to carnivores is called a food chain.

CHAINED TO YOUR FOOD

You are part of many food chains. Can you work out three food chains of which you are part, one involving popcorn, one with milk, and one with eggs? One of the chains has only two links—which is it?

An ocean food chain involving sea otters

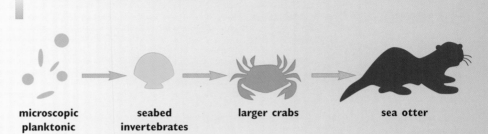

microscopic planktonic algae → seabed invertebrates → larger crabs → sea otter

ADAPTING TO THE DIET

Animals have special adaptations to help them eat their normal food. For instance, it is hard to extract nutrients from plants, so herbivores have a long digestive system to help them get the maximum benefit from their food.

Plants cannot run away, but a carnivore's food (its prey) may escape or fight back. A carnivore needs to kill quickly, or else the prey may escape or wound its attacker. Lions kill their prey quickly by biting the neck with their dagger-like canine teeth. Crocodiles often drag their prey into water and drown them to cut short the struggle and save energy.

This is a photo of a spider mite taken under a microscope.

BIOLOGICAL CONTROL

It has been found that the numbers of certain pests can be controlled by introducing a predator into their habitat. For example, the spider mite is a spider-like pest that can damage greenhouse crops. If mites that prey on spider mites are introduced into the greenhouse, the number of spider mites is reduced without having to use pesticides. Controlling pests using a predator is called biological control.

FROM FOOD CHAIN TO FOOD WEB

There are many food chains in a habitat, and they all link together to form a food web.

By studying food webs, ecologists have discovered that if one link is removed from one food chain in a web, organisms in other parts of the habitat can be affected. For example, sea otters live on the Pacific coast in parts of North America. A feature of this habitat is forests of kelp growing in the water. At one time, sea otter numbers went down, and large areas of kelp forest disappeared. The reason for this was that the sea otters fed on sea urchins, which ate the kelp. When there were fewer sea otters to eat the sea urchins, the urchins' numbers increased and they destroyed the kelp.

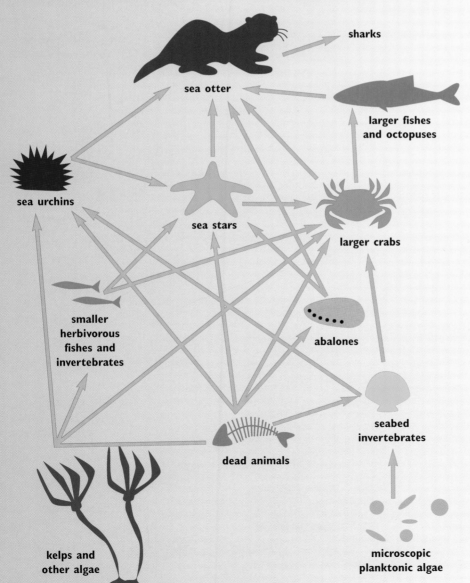

sharks

sea otter

larger fishes and octopuses

sea urchins

sea stars

larger crabs

smaller herbivorous fishes and invertebrates

abalones

dead animals

seabed invertebrates

kelps and other algae

microscopic planktonic algae

Rachel Carson (1907–1964), an American biologist, studied food chains and how they were affected by pesticides (chemicals used to destroy animals that attack crops). She wrote a book in which she showed how the careless use of pesticides could lead to the destruction of other animals that were not pests. For example, songbirds could eat insects that had taken in pesticides and become poisoned too. The birds would no longer be there to sing in the spring— hence the title of her book, *Silent Spring*.

Carson's book made people aware of the dangers of pesticides. This has led to laws being made in many countries to control pesticide use.

WRITE ABOUT A HABITAT

Write about a place such as your local park or some natural habitat you know, and explain why it should not be replaced by houses or factories.

RECYCLING TO SURVIVE

Animals feed and make wastes, and many organisms die rather than being eaten, so why is the world not littered with manure and dead bodies? The answer is found in the soil.

Many people think of soil as just dirt, but in fact it is a habitat on which all other habitats depend. Most wastes and dead bodies come to rest on the soil. There the materials from which they are made are broken down into simple minerals. This breakdown of the wastes and bodies is called decomposition. The simple minerals produced by decomposition can be absorbed by plants—this is called recycling. Without these two processes, life on Earth would have ended long ago. A wide range of organisms survive by recycling materials.

One way we can recycle waste food and plant materials from the house and garden is to make compost.

MICROBES

When bacteria or fungi land on dead bodies and wastes, they begin to feed. To do this, they produce chemicals that break down the tissues of the animal or plant. We call this rotting. The bacteria that cause rotting are too small to see, but their effects can be seen. The threads of a fungus usually grow within the dead organism, but some fungi make large, spore-producing structures we call mushrooms or toadstools.

BURYING BEETLES

Burying beetles can detect rotting flesh from a long way off. When a pair of beetles finds the body of a mouse or a small bird, they dig out the soil below it until it sinks into the ground. The female beetle then lays her eggs in a tunnel close to the buried body. When the eggs hatch, the beetle larvae feed on the dead body.

Bracket fungi are a kind of toadstool that feed on tree stumps and dead wood.

DUNG BEETLES

Dung beetles feed on manure. They mold the manure into a ball, roll it away, bury it, and then feed on it. They also lay eggs in the balls of manure and then bury them. When the larvae hatch, they feed on the manure as they grow.

EARTHWORMS

Soil contains a mixture of rocks and material from wastes and decomposed bodies. As earthworms move through the soil, they eat it. They absorb some of the material from living things, and the rest of the soil passes through their bodies. This breaks the soil up into fine pieces. Earthworms also make burrows in the soil, which lets in air so that other decomposers in the soil can breathe.

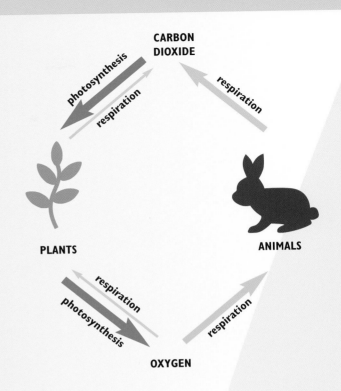

FINDING EARTHWORMS

Are there any earthworms in a grassy area near you? Pour some water over an area of grass the size of a bath towel, then tap the edge with your foot. After a few minutes, earthworms should appear on the surface.

SWAPPING WASTES

Both plants and animals get energy through respiration (see page 4). Carbon dioxide is a waste product, but during the day, plants use this carbon dioxide, plus more carbon dioxide from the air, to make food by photosynthesis. The waste product of photosynthesis is oxygen, so by day, plants release oxygen into the air. This oxygen is used by other living things when they breathe.

HELPING PLANT GROWTH

Justus von Leibig (1803–1873), a German chemist, investigated which materials were taken from soil by plants. He found that the materials were simple chemicals that we call minerals. He found that by adding these chemicals to the soil, plants would grow well. His work led to the production of fertilizers, which contain the minerals that plants need to grow.

BIOMES AND COMMUNITIES

Different communities of plants and animals live in different parts of the world. The plants and animals that live in each area are adapted to the environmental conditions there—how hot or cold it is, and how much rain falls. They are also adapted to live with each other and form food chains and webs. Large areas that have broadly similar communities of plants and animals are called biomes. The major biomes are described below.

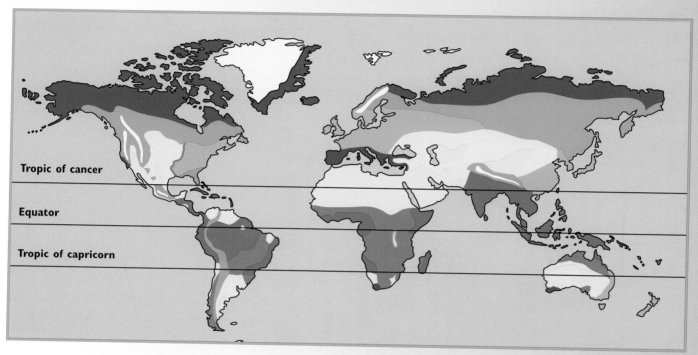

Tropic of cancer

Equator

Tropic of capricorn

POLAR REGIONS

The very low temperatures and long periods of darkness in polar regions mean that few plants grow there. Most animals there, such as seals, polar bears, and penguins, get their food from the ocean around them.

 ## TUNDRA

Tundra regions are cold all year, but in the summer, the ground near the surface thaws out, and thick vegetation of grass and lichens develops. Reindeer, musk ox, arctic hares, and lemmings eat the grass and lichens, while wolves and snowy owls hunt animals.

 ## CONIFEROUS FOREST

Cool summers followed by snowy winters provide conditions for the growth of huge numbers of conifers. Moose and squirrels are common herbivores, while lynx and martens (large relatives of weasels) are key predators of smaller mammals.

 ## TEMPERATE FOREST

Cool winters and warm summers provide conditions for woods and forests of deciduous, broad-leaved trees. These trees provide homes for beetles and other insects, which are eaten by birds such as woodpeckers. Deer are larger herbivores, while foxes are common carnivores.

RAIN FOREST

The hot, wet conditions at certain places around the equator allow huge rain forests of tall trees to grow. Each of the rain forest regions has its own distinctive plants and animals. For example, howler monkeys are found in the Amazon rain forest, while gorillas are found in the African rain forests.

TROPICAL GRASSLAND

Generally, warm weather with wet and dry seasons provides conditions for open grasslands dotted with trees. Gazelles, antelopes, and zebras are the main herbivores. They are hunted by lions, leopards, cheetahs, and hyenas.

TEMPERATE GRASSLAND

In temperate areas where it is too dry for forests, large areas of grassland form. Bison and pronghorn graze on the North American prairies, while saiga antelope roam the steppes of Asia. Wolves are the largest carnivores on the steppes, while on the prairies, coyotes eat smaller prey and carrion.

DESERT

Deserts are areas with very little rainfall. Many plants survive only as seeds during the driest time of the year, while plants such as cacti survive by storing water. Most desert animals hide in burrows during the day and come out to eat at night.

OCEANS

Huge areas of salty water cover almost three-quarters of Earth's surface. Light penetrates only a little way through the ocean's surface, so most marine plant life is located near the surface. Animals such as fish, mollusks, and crustaceans live both near the surface and much deeper.

SCRUBLAND

Scrubland forms in areas with hot summers and mild winters. The land is covered with aromatic (strong-smelling) evergreen bushes. Scrublands support many types of animals, including seed-eating rodents, insects, and reptiles.

NATURE PROTECTION

In Africa, many familiar animals such as lions, giraffes, and elephants are found in large numbers only in protected national parks.

In many biomes, huge portions of the natural community have been destroyed to make way for towns and farms. Many species are in danger of becoming extinct. Nature reserves have been set up in many places to protect the wildlife.

TIMELINE

Aristotle (384–322 B.C.), a Greek scientist, observed many living things and tried to arrange them in order according to their features.

Jan Baptista van Helmont (A.D. 1580–1644), a Flemish (Belgian) scientist, showed that water and some materials in the soil were needed for plant growth.

Francesco Redi (1626–1697), an Italian doctor, showed that living things did not develop from non-living material through his work with maggots and rotting meat.

Antonie van Leeuwenhoek (1632–1723), a Dutch biologist, built small but powerful microscopes that he used to see protists and bacteria.

Robert Hooke (1635–1703), an English scientist, introduced the word "cell" to describe the tiny structures from which living things are made.

Carolus Linnaeus (1707–1778), a Swedish botanist, set up a way of grouping or classifying living things that is still used today.

Jan Ingenhousz (1730–1799), a Dutch scientist, showed that plants need carbon dioxide from the air to make food.

Robert Brown (1773–1858), a Scottish scientist, named the dark spot in a cell the "nucleus."

Justus von Liebig (1803–1873), a German chemist, discovered that plants need minerals from the soil for healthy growth.

Gregor Mendel (1822–1884), an Austrian monk, made many experiments on how pea plants reproduce and found that instructions were passed from one generation to the next.

Karl von Frisch (1886–1982), an Austrian zoologist, discovered that bees communicate information to each other about where nectar-producing flowers can be found.

Rachel Carson (1907–1964), an American biologist, wrote about how pesticides pass through food chains. Her work led to the more careful use of pesticides in many countries.

GLOSSARY

amphibian – an animal such as a frog or toad with a skeleton of bone, skin without scales or hair, and young called tadpoles.

bacteria – very small, single-celled living things with no DNA inside the nucleus.

biome – a large area with similar types of plants and animals. An example is the temperate forest biome.

carbon dioxide – a gas produced by respiration.

carnivore – an animal that eats other animals.

carrion – when an animal feeds on a dead body that is rotting, the meat is called carrion.

chloroplasts – a tiny, green part of a plant cell that absorbs energy from sunlight to make food.

GLOSSARY (continued)

crustacean – an animal such as a crab, shrimp, or lobster. Its body is covered in a jointed shell that allows the movement of the back and limbs.

deciduous – a tree or bush that loses all its leaves at one time during the year (either in winter or during a dry season).

DNA – material from which our genes are made. DNA molecules contain a code that instructs cells on how they should grow and develop.

embryo – a very young living thing before it hatches, is born, or sprouts from a seed.

excretion – the release of waste substances from the body due to life processes such as respiration.

fungi – living things such as mushrooms and molds. Many fungi are microbes, and they feed on dead or living plants and animals.

gametes – reproductive cells.

genetic material – the DNA inside the nucleus of cells, which carries information about how a living thing should grow and develop.

herbivores – animals that eat only plants for food.

larva (pl. larvae) – the stage in an insect's life cycle between the egg and the pupa, and between the egg and the adult for amphibians.

lichens – plant-like living things that are often found growing on the surface of rocks or tree trunks.

mammals – animals such as mice, humans, and bears. Most give birth to live babies, and the young feed on milk from their mothers.

minerals – simple chemicals in the soil that plants and animals need for healthy growth.

mollusks – animals such as snails that do not have a backbone. Their fleshy body is usually protected by one or two shells.

nectar – a sugary liquid produced by flowers to attract insects.

nutrients – substances in food and in soil that a living thing needs for energy, growth, and good health.

omnivores – animals that feed on both plants and animals.

ovules – the parts of a flower that contain the egg cells. After fertilization, they change into seeds.

protists – living things (micro-organisms) with bodies made from a single cell.

reptiles – animals such as crocodiles that have scaly skin and lay eggs on land.

respiration – the process of releasing energy from food to the cells in the body by taking in oxygen and giving out carbon dioxide.

spores – a microscopic case containing living material from a fungus, moss, or fern that is used in the organism's reproduction.

stamen – part of the flower in which pollen grains are made.

stigma – part of the flower that collects pollen from insects or air currents.

xylem – cells that form tubes in plants to transport water.

zygote – the cell produced after an egg cell has been fertilized.

INDEX

2